Interpretation of

Lessons in Truth

by
Charles Roth

Cover artwork by Marilyn Roth

Published by
Newview Publications
Pasadena, California

To order more copies of this book go to
Lulu.com or Amazon.com

ISBN 978-1-304-15899-4

INTRODUCTION

The chapters in this booklet were originally written to teach the classic and basic Unity book LESSONS IN TRUTH, by H. Emily Cady to a radio audience of thousands in a mini-network of stations including Chicago, Buffalo, Indianapolis and many more.

Using our present-day vocabulary and "for instances" helped to simplify and make clearer the ageless principles, and therefore more usable to radio listeners not familiar with Unity's practical approach to the teachings of Jesus.

I trust that you, the individual reader will find help in its pages – you certainly will find my love and prayers invisibly tucked behind or within the words.

Charles Roth

CONTENTS

BONDAGE OR LIBERTY, WHICH?

Lesson One

The time has come for man to awaken to the fact that his bondage – or his liberty – is not DEPENDENT on his outer environment. This awakening does not happen easily because we have been programmed from birth to DEPEND on outer conditions and people for our support, well-being, and happiness.

What you depend on, you become enslaved to. So we have become enslaved to, in bondage to our outer environment with its conditions and people. It becomes a vicious circle. You try to break out of your bondage by grasping for more outer things such as money or position and putting our faith in, or depending on them and you find yourself right back in bondage again because, what you depend on, you become enslaved to.

The answer is not in the outer, through legislation or force, or through a bottle or a change of scenery. These give temporary relief, at best. The answer to the trials and tribulations of life is found within.

The age is dawning when man is discovering the tremendous pent-up Power within him. Discovering the life-changing truth in the statement of John, " . . . for he who is in you is greater than he who is in the world." (I John 4:4)

Greater is the Power within each individual than the seeming power of conditions and environments. If this is not true, then we should add an appendage to the Bible saying something to the effect that the Bible is helpful and effective in many cases, but that there are other cases where the power of appearances, the power of outer conditions is greater than the power that the Bible speaks of.

But I say that with my tongue in cheek, of course. Deep within we all KNOW that God's Spirit within man is greater than any outer seeming power. Our problem, our need is to learn how to effectively contact and release that miracle-working Power into our lives. And that is what we intend to do in this series – at least, to take some long strides in that direction.

The Bible is your instruction Book. As you read the lines and in between the lines, you will find that it was written especially for you, and about you.

For instance, in Exodus 3:7, you read:

> *"Then the Lord said, I have seen the affliction of my people who are in Egypt, and have heard their cry because of their taskmasters; I know their sufferings, and I have come down to deliver them out of the hand of the Egyptians, and you bring them up out of that land to a good and broad land, a land flowing with milk and honey."*

Do you see yourself in that ancient passage? Egypt represents the darkness of ignorance of whom and what we are as spiritual beings, as children of God, as channels of expression of the universal Life and Love and Power and Wisdom and All-potentiality of God!

In other words, we think we are "just" human beings. Physical bodies containing a mind which enables us to think and a heart that makes us tick. We think of ourselves as relatively powerless and limited. To become more powerful we look to things like college degrees, money, and position. And lacking these things we feel we are limited, doomed to a lower place in the universal caste system.

Infinite Intelligence is saying through the passage in Exodus that It or He is aware of your plight. Your sobbing into your pillow in the privacy of your bed is heard. God knows that life for you is tough, and He wants to help. But the first move is up to you. You must reach out.

When you do, Infinite Intelligence will easily, effortlessly, and when it calls for it, miraculously, lead you out of your Egyptian darkness of pain and suffering, to a land or a life flowing with milk and honey – which, of course, means a life of fulfillment, of meaning, of happiness you never dreamed attainable.

Read the story of the Children of Israel following Moses out of Egypt again. It is the story of your own unfoldment from a caterpillar to butterfly – or from a limited human being to an unlimited human-divine being!

It begins with the Children of Israel in Egypt. This is you, a child of God, in the darkness of ignorance that you ARE a Child of God.

The Israelites, after a lot of stalling, arguing, and procrastinating listen to Moses. Moses represents Law, spiritual Law. In other words, you or me, finally stop arguing about the outer trappings of religion, stop complaining about our troubles and bad luck and admit that there is a Higher Law that governs and directs the universe and everything in it from the exact swing of the stars to the predictable behavior of an atom. And that our access to that Higher Law is from within.

Moses said he represented whom; "I Am," didn't he? When Moses asked God who he should tell the Children of Israel sent him, the answer was "I Am that I Am. Tell them I Am sent you."

So Moses, or that which leads you, a child of God, out of your suffering and unhappiness, is found within you – in the recesses of that core of your being that continually whispers. I AM!

As you have faith in and follow the guidance of that inner Leader you find things working out for you in a wonderful way. When the Egyptian taskmasters of sorrow, sickness, or lack seem about to overtake you – the Red Sea miraculously opens for you – and closes behind you. You find your daily manna, or supply for your present needs, is always provided. However, if you slip into consciousness and get greedy – you soon find that manna cannot be stored up or withheld. The Children of Israel found yesterday's manna moldy.

> *"Sometime, somewhere, every human being must come to himself. Having tired of eating husks, he will 'arise and go to my father,' to quote the prodigal son."*

You who are listening and I have already come to ourselves. We have had enough of cowering to conditions that threaten and scare us. Enough of the shame of helplessness. We have started out on the journey that all are destined to take – the journey from Egypt to the land of liberty.

There will come times when we think we can go it alone and start to fashion and worship a "golden calf." But it is a funny thing about the journey of Truth – there is no turning back.

Then, too, there may come wilderness experiences when our courage seems to fail. Times like those when Moses had to tell the trembling Children of Israel, "Fear not, stand firm, and see the salvation of the Lord, which he will work for you." (Exodus 14:13)

We, too, must remember that our help comes from within. True power over ourselves and conditions comes out of quiet moments of meditation.

You might begin with some simple statement of Truth. Find a private and quiet place. Make yourself comfortable and then close your eyes and dwell in the land of consciousness within.

> Say, or think, "I am much more than this physical body that I am wearing or inhabiting. This physical body is an ingenious, complex aggregation of atoms. This body is only about 2% of me – the other 98% is mental and spiritual.

> "From the spiritual phase of my being comes the Life that animates and enlivens my body, the Power that enables me to think and to feel.

> "I am connected to and one with the universal Life and Spirit that enlivens and indwells all persons. We call this universal Creative Spirit God, and so I am one with God.

> "As I acknowledge and realize and accept the Truth of oneness with God, I become a part of the underlying harmony and perfection and power which God is. I become the outlet through which formless and all-potential Spirit flows into outer form as beauty, order, and the fulfillment of my every need."

You see, sooner or later each of us must stand alone with our indwelling God. Life is an individual matter. We cannot enter the consciousness of the kingdom of God collectively – either through legislation, or church membership. There is a land of the fulfillment for you and me – we walk toward it together, but yet alone.

So, which will it be BONDAGE OR LIBERTY? Go it alone, if you so choose. There is a Spiritual Reality in or to this universe. You can ignore it or laugh at it or argue about it and continue to chafe in your chains.

Or you can take your first step out bondage by affirming:

> "GOD IS AND I AM
> AND GOD IS THAT I AM!"

STATEMENT OF BEING

Lesson Two

Chapter Two is entitled STATEMENT OF BEING. Its purpose is to introduce what to many people is a new concept of God – the concept of God as Spirit.

And right here we find the first place where Unity leaves the path taken by traditional Christianity. Traditional Christianity has always implied, if not taught, the concept of God as a Person.

Think about this in your own life. When your mother had you say your bedtime prayers as a child, didn't you pray as if you were having a private conversation with a Divine Person some place up in the sky?

In your formative years you ran into pictures of God painted by Renaissance painters. Pictures showing an old man with a flowing beard and a grave expression on His face – surrounded by angels with wings growing out of their backs – and the background always suggested the locale as high in the sky.

Most of the hymns that you sang talked in terms of God as a Person. As a King, perhaps, who sat on a throne and watched over the activities of people on earth and from His supreme vantage point dispensed justice, sometimes in the form of rewards, sometimes in the form of punishment.

Now, it might be said that a child cannot conceive of an abstract concept such as that of God as Spirit. A child's mind can only comprehend something concrete and so for a child to pray to God as a Person is normal and perhaps necessary. I will go along with that. Although, the children in a Unity Sunday School do pretty well at thinking of God as within them and all around them.

But even if we did need a "God with skin on" as one child put it, when we were a child; there should come a time when we are old enough to be told that Jesus described the God He worshipped as Spirit!

One of the most significant, and yet one of the most overlooked passages in the teachings of Jesus is in the fourth chapter of John where Jesus is talking to the Samaritan woman at the well and reveals to her His concept of the true nature of God.

The Samaritans and the Jews were kind of rivals, religion-wise. The Samaritans believed in the same God as the Jews. But the Samaritans firmly believed that God dwelled on a mountain in Samaria, while the Jews just as firmly believed that God dwelt in Jerusalem, in the Temple, behind the veil in the Holy of Holies.

When the Samaritan woman mentioned this rivalry, Jesus answered, in effect, "God is Spirit; everywhere present Spirit. God isn't only and exclusively in the Temple in Jerusalem, or on your mountain in Samaria. Because God is everywhere present Spirit you or anyone can worship Him in Spirit and in Truth anywhere, at any time!"

This, then, is the basic foundation of Unity's interpretation of the teachings of Jesus – that God is invisible, everywhere present, always and instantly accessible SPIRIT!

And so in this chapter on the STATEMENT OF BEING, Dr. Cady is suggesting that we abandon the concept of God as the Superhuman Person we conceived Him to be as a child; and to explore the rich field of understanding that opens up to us when we think of God in terms of everywhere present, all-potential Spirit – as Jesus taught.

Well, let's explore together.

First, what is Spirit? What do we mean by Spirit?

Spirit comes from a Latin word "Spiritus," which means to breathe, to blow. Breath is Life. God is Spirit and Spirit is Life. Therefore God is Life; the very Life which is leading you right now and enabling you to stay, "I am," or "I am alive," or "I am a vehicle of Life!"

This is why we speak of Unity as a PRACTICAL interpretation of the teachings of Jesus. You will find it extremely practical in maintaining your health of body, or in accelerating the healing process if you are ill – if in meditation you realize that God is the very Life which is flowing through you. As you open your mind to this basic Truth of you being the very cells and atoms of your physical garment of flesh respond.

Doctors today readily admit the power of negative and destructive emotions and thoughts to hurt and destroy the body. What is needed is the insight to see that this works two ways – positive and constructive emotions and thoughts release a creative Power that rebuilds and renews the body. And when the feelings and thoughts are oriented around a statement of the Truth that God's perfect Life is flowing through you – a tremendous healing Power is released. For example:

*"I AM ONE WITH THE UNIVERSAL LIFE
OF GOD. IT IS FLOWING THROUGH ME
NOW. I FEEL IT, AND I AM BEING MADE
WHOLE, PRAISE GOD!"*

But God, or Spirit, is much more than a healing Presence and Power. God or Spirit has attributes. An attribute, according to Webster is: "A characteristic or quality of thing." Dr. Cady lists the following attributes, or characteristics or qualities inherent in Spirit:

LIFE   POWER   WISDOM   SUBSTANCE   LOVE

What this means in practical terms is that no matter what the needs, no matter what the problem or challenge, Spirit has inherent within it a Principle that will lead to the answer to that problem, the fulfillment of that need.

If healing is the need, Spirit flows forth through you as Life – restorative, revitalizing Life. If guidance is the need, the attribute of Wisdom enlightens your mind with understanding and reveals the right action to take. If there is inharmony in your home, your work, your personal relationships, Love is the attribute or quality that responds to your call and expresses in your world as harmony, unity, adjustment.

This is why we describe God as All-potential. Because whatever your need, no matter how impossible it may seem to you, the fulfillment is possible when you appeal to Spirit with its Superhuman qualities.

> You may say, "if it is that simple why doesn't God answer my prayers?"

Well, it is simple: but it isn't easy. God or Spirit requires your full and complete trust and dependence in order to function freely through you and for you. We find it difficult to give this. We may want to, but wanting to do something and doing it are two different things as you well know.

First of all, it is understandably difficult to trust in and depend on something intangible to the five senses, when the problem is so very visible and tangible! The problem circumstances hypnotize us, in a sense, so that we can't take our eyes and our attention off of it. All we can think of or talk about is this terrible problem and the mind races on to all the possible dire consequences if the problem doesn't go away right soon.

I think "hypnotizes" is the right word, because it seems that even after we have been reminded of the Truth that God is the answer, but that God requires our complete faith and dependence – we still compulsively go back to stewing and fretting and rehashing our problem.

For instance, someone will call me for spiritual help in regard to some painful challenge. After listening to the problem for few minutes I will try to remind them of the Truth of God's Presence, Power, willingness and ability to work things out. They will agree, but all too often they then continue to explain how awful it is, how much they have suffered, how unfair the other person has been or whatever.

It might seem unsympathetic to stop them, but it is the only loving thing to do if you want to help. Dwelling on the problem only cuts off the help, the spiritual help that he so desperately needed.

You can see why I said that receiving God's help is simple, but not easy. It is simple in that all we need to do is turn to God and depend completely on His ability, His power, and His wisdom to bring about a right solution. I am purposely using the word "depend" because it carries much more weight or meaning or responsibility than the words "trust" or "have faith in." We can say that we have faith in God, but then find ourselves feeling that our solution DEPENDS on a certain person changing his mind, or a certain way to open up. We then are depending on our outer power instead of the One Power.

Well, let's sum up this chapter by saying that the basic premise upon which you build a new spiritually oriented life is this:

> God is Spirit, and you are an emanation or
> expression of that one universal Spirit.

The word "expression" means a "pressing out." You are a center of consciousness through which God is continually "pressing out." The extent to which God "presses out" into your body as health and into your world as harmony, prosperity, and order is contingent on you providing the most favorable mental conditions – and those most favorable mental conditions are what? Depending on the invisible presence and power of God exclusively – which means not giving any power, any credence, or any faith (which means fear) to the changing, changeable outer conditions.

Not easy, is it? But that is only because we are not accustomed to living that way. Start now and you will find it gets easier each time you exercise your control over your thoughts and feelings and choose to depend on God.

THINKING

Lesson Three

In the last lesson we discussed the point that God is not to be thought of as a Man – sitting on a throne high in the sky, attended by a bevy of angels.

God is Spirit, Jesus taught. Universal Spirit, everywhere present, always present Spirit. Invisible, yes; but very real. Let's pause for a moment here to convince ourselves that difficult though it may be, we can and we do believe in and completely trust things that are invisible. How about radio waves? Who of us would deny that these invisible waves transmit sound across miles – even to the moon and back?

Or take the atom. Scientists tell us that our bodies and indeed all things are made up of tiny swirling atoms. Nobody has ever seen an atom, but we certainly have totally accepted the belief that they exist.

It probably wasn't easy for people to accept the idea of invisible radio waves and invisible atoms; but when they first listened to a crystal set radio, or saw pictures of the atom bomb going off this helped them to believe it very quickly.

God is universal Spirit and invisible to the sense of sight. And just as the explosion proved the existence of the invisible atom, or the voice of an announcer in New York City coming over your radio proves the existence of invisible radio waves, so does the easily seen order of the universe, the intricate and orderly design of the human body or a snowflake or a blade of grass, prove the existence of an invisible but Causitive Intelligence.

Once we are able to grasp the fact that God is – that we are not praying to an empty room, nor to a Person in the sky who may or may not be listening – then we are ready to seek out our own personal relationship to this universal Spirit. Perhaps It is in the intelligent First Cause behind the precise swing of the planets and the orderly unfolding of a rose bud; but what is Its relationship to you?

Dr. Cady explained the relationship of God's universal Spirit to you in a beautiful analogy. She writes:

> "Imagine if you will, a great reservoir, out of which lead innumerable small rivulets or channels. At its farther end each channel opens out into a small fountain. This fountain is not only being continually filled and replenished from the reservoir but is itself a radiating center whence it gives out in all directions that which it receives, so that all who come within its radius are refreshed and blessed.
>
> "This is our relation to God. Each one of us is a radiating center. Each one, no matter how small or ignorant, is the little fountain at the far end of the channel, the other end of which leads out from all there is in God. This fountain represents the individuality, as separate from the great reservoir, God; and yet as one with Him in that we are constantly fed and renewed from Him, and without Him we are nothing."

Isn't this a tremendous thought! You, perhaps, always thought you were a nothing – just a name in a telephone book, a number in the Social Security computer bank. You depended upon your education to get you a good job, you depended on other people liking you or being interested in you (which really means, being able to use you) in order to advance in the world. You depended upon your intellectual cunning and secret planning to maneuver people and circumstances into situations that would be favorable to your well-being.

But now comes this life-changing thought that the Intelligence that created and sustains the orderly and unfathomable universe has an outlet, or finds a point of expression IN YOU.

What need is there then to DEPEND on outer people or circumstances with all the worry, fear, tension, disappointment, and anxiety that such dependence involves. Why not DEPEND on that within you which is All-wise, All-powerful, always present, and always available.

But, as you and I know, this is easier said than done. There is one factor that universal Intelligence has designed into Its creation, Man, that has been our downfall. This factor is our FREEDOM OF CHOICE.

Without this factor of FREEDOM OF CHOICE we would be robots, or we might say, vegetables in human form. The faculty of Freedom of Choice keeps us in bondage when we use it to depend on outer people, conditions and events; but that same faculty is our deliverance when we use it to choose to depend on universal Mind, universal Spirit, or God as It or He finds a personalized point of expression in us.

Let's take a moment to see how this actually works in practice; for instance, in a healing challenge.

You become aware of some physical symptoms that are unusual; perhaps nausea or dizziness or fever or whatever. You start thinking about medical columns you have read, about these symptoms, or perhaps T.V. public service spots sponsored by Heart Societies or the numerous other Societies that graphically enumerate tell-tale symptoms of sickness and disease.

You're thinking arouses feeling; and naturally the feeling isn't going to be a good feeling. It is going to be a "feeling" of fear or apprehension, of anxiety. You go to a doctor and he acknowledges the validity of the symptoms and gives a diagnosis.

You'll obediently followed directions and depending upon the doctors skill, or luck, or whatever, you either get better or not.

Say you get better. Your body is better off, but you as a person are not. You live in fear of another illness or a reoccurrence. You feel helpless and alone and utterly dependent upon pills and medicine for your health.

But now take a person who takes control of his Freedom of Choice when he finds physical symptoms that are unusual. He doesn't necessarily deny them or say that they don't exist. Rather he says to himself, "Which has more power, the symptoms and whatever bugs are causing them; or God's Spirit in me?"

And he answers himself, "God's Spirit has more power without a doubt!"

But then he thinks to himself, "Well, what are we going to do about the symptoms?" And the answer comes back, "Let God within, the Light of Understanding guide you into the correct action."

After a quiet period of meditative prayer he feels that seeing a doctor is the wise thing to do. As he follows through with his feeling he sees the doctor as a child of God also, he knows that universal Wisdom works through any and all channels and so he obeys the doctor's suggestions – not with trepidation, fear and crossed fingers, but with calmness, patience and serenity. You see, the dependence is still on God, and he is grateful for and to whatever instrument God uses to bring his good to him in this case renewed health.

I trust that this hypothetical illustration points out the fact that CHOOSING TO DEPEND ON GOD does not mean ignoring the world with its people, conditions, and events. It merely means seeing them in a larger perspective. It means seeing them and yourself as instruments of the Divine Movement or the Divine Power, and not as a Power in themselves.

When you think of people or conditions as having power in themselves you are afraid of them, you depend on their favor, you are in bondage to them. But when you think of them as instruments of a higher Power whose essential nature is good, beneficial – then there is no fear, no sense of bondage, no sense of helpless dependency. And most important of all, you remain calm, patient, and serene within yourself.

Thought is formative. Thought shapes and molds your environment and your future. "As he (man) thinketh in his heart so is he."

But more important than knowledge of the formative power of thought is the knowledge that the inborn faculty of Freedom of Choice directs the awesome formative power of thought.

And to trace it back farther than that we could say that DESIRE influences the way we will use our faculty of Freedom of Choice. Until you deeply and powerfully desire to DEPEND on God, until that becomes not just a hobby, or a one day a week distraction from the monotonous business of daily life – but becomes a driving and all-consuming desire, well, you will find yourself looking at the outer world of facts, then contemplating for an instant the intangible, seemingly theoretical, invisible presence of Universal Spirit or – God and choosing to go along with the facts – choosing to depend on outer things and people that you can watch, observe, and maneuver or influence when you feel it is necessary.

To put it briefly and starkly: we would rather play god – be god ourselves, than throw aside all of our learning and position and hard-learned ability to manipulate people and completely trust a God we can't see or check up on or demand explanations from. Our ego doesn't like being Number Two; and that is just what we have to be if we are to completely DEPEND ON GOD.

Let's close the lesson with a practical suggestion for helping you to choose to DEPEND on God at all times, but most especially when you are in big trouble that your intellect finds too hot to handle.

First, of course, there has to be desire. And that is up to you. But if you truly, deeply desire to DEPEND on God, then when trouble rears its ugly face and facts, think of the radio waves. Turn on your radio and note how you believe in invisible radio waves. Look at your hands. They are actually millions of atoms swirling around, invisible, but lumped together they give the appearance of a hand.

> *Then say to yourself, if I can believe these invisible phenomena, I can and I will believe in the very real presence and power of God, and I WILL DEPEND ON THAT POWER TO GUIDE ME THROUGH THIS CHALLENGE TO MY GREATER GOOD.*

DENIALS

Lesson Four

DENIAL is an essential tool in chipping away at the crystalized, false beliefs which we have allowed to encrust our soul and cover over the Light that eternally shines from within.

Some Truth students resist the idea of DENIAL, feeling that to deny something admits its existence and thereby gives it power.

This isn't necessarily true. The factor that gives it power is your fear of it, or your own belief that it has power. For instance, if a fly should light on your hand you would admit its existence, and you would calmly shoo it away. But if someone would falsely tell you that the fly carried a dreaded disease that resulted in quick death – you would become panic-stricken with fear. The very same fly – but your complete belief that it had death in its soft touch gives it power to quicken your heartbeat and make you turn ashen with fear.

Acknowledging the fly doesn't give it power to frighten you. Your false belief that the fly is deadly gives it power to frighten you.

This is the basis of Black Magic or Voodoo. A pin stuck in a doll is just a pin stuck in a doll; but if you were reared in a culture that programmed you into believing that a certain person sticking a pin into a doll while repeating incantations would affect you in a destructive way – well, it would!

The point is, that it is your belief that gives a thing power. And so what a knowledgeable Truth student denies is his own ignorantly accepted false beliefs.

Let's take for instance a false belief that you are inferior to other people. Of course such a belief doesn't come right up and shout to you, "Here I am, a belief that you are inferior to others!"

It might try to say that, if you would let it, but the vain ego doesn't like to face such a painful fact, so it disguises or masks that belief with a more acceptable costume. Excuses such as, "If I had a better education, or if I had the opportunities others had I would be as good as they are!" You see, that makes you feel better, but it doesn't make you BETTER, it makes you WORSE: because these excuses foster feelings of resentment or jealously or hostility toward others and these in turn, lead you to guilt, greater unhappiness, unpopularity, misfortune and you make up more justifications for your misery and failure.

As you progress in your study of Truth you discover how necessary it is, and how painful it is to be honest with yourself, and humble.

In times of quiet meditation, if you face your inner thoughts and feelings calmly and unemotionally and don't try to excuse them or dismiss them from mind . . . you will see your misbehavior or wrong behavior. And revealed, too, will be the false belief that caused you to act wrongly.

Then you are in a position to work on that wrong belief with the principle of DENIAL.

This is the deeper and true meaning of REPENTANCE. But most people don't feel they have anything to be repentant about – what they actually MEAN is that they have a good "excuse" or a good "reason" for any action or feeling that the inner Light reveals to be wrong.

So, let's say you are ready to cut out the excuses, to stop the vanity-prompted justifications and to get at the real culprit – the false belief that you are inferior to other people.

But first let me give you a little salve for the wounded ego. Don't feel so badly about having or harboring this false belief in your inferiority because it isn't your belief, you didn't create it, it doesn't belong to you at all – it is something someone gave you and you accepted!

Perhaps when you were a child you underwent a traumatic experience such as having to sit in a special section for the dull children because you misspelled more than ten out of a hundred words. The teacher, the system, the experience is strongly suggesting to your suggestible mind that you are pretty stupid – duller than others, inferior to others. That, plus additional reinforcing suggestions that you are inferior – such as being turned down as a cheerleader, perhaps getting fired from your first job – they all add up until you are really convinced of your inferiority and you totally accept that false belief which, as I said wasn't your idea in the first place – it was something someone else gave you, purposely or unwittingly, and you accepted.

So don't feel too badly about this feeling of inferiority. It is something that you, like millions of others, inadvertently picked up without realizing it. Now, the point is to get rid of it.

Here, then, is where DENIAL comes in. When you are faced with a task or a circumstance that aroused that old feeling of "I can't," or "I'm afraid," or "What excuse can I give to get out of this?" recognize that feeling of dread and fear as THAT OLD FALSE BELIEF that you are inferior to others. Then destroy it, chop away at it, with the principle of DENIAL by saying and thinking until you FEEL it, "I am not afraid!" "I am not inferior to others;" "It is not true that I am not good enough!"

This, you see, is acknowledging the false belief of inferiority; but it is not giving it power, because you are not afraid of it. You see it for what it is – something someone handed to you, and you in ignorance accepted it, kept it, and foolishly came to think that it was always yours. Now the Light of Understanding reveals the truth about it. It is merely a hypnotic suggestion from the outer world – and once you shake off the hypnotic suggestion you can see what a "patsy" you were to ever believe it – and it has no more power to compel you to dance to its tune.

Hypnotism is a big word. It covers a lot of territory. Kreskin, one of the country's leading hypnotists, at a public lecture here in Indianapolis flatly stated that there is no such thing as a hypnotic trance. He said that the human mind is tremendously suggestible at all times. We are continually accepting suggestions through ads, newspapers, speakers, books, relatives, teachers, doctors, and whole spectrum of outer experience.

A hypnotist merely works with or on the subject's already-present suggestibility. This is why they say that they do not "make" a subject do anything; it is the subject's own choice. That is, the subject accepted the suggestion.

The way to avoid being influenced, motivated, hypnotized, programmed (whichever word you want to use) by your outer environment is to live in a consciousness of the Light of Truth within you, and to hold all that your outer senses report to you up to the judgment of that Inner Light. Then you are truly "thinking for yourself," or more precisely, you are letting God think through you.

This is the meaning of that passage in John, "Judge not according to the appearance, but judge righteous judgment." (John 7:24) Many people think to themselves (although they seldom dare say it), "How do you judge righteous judgment?" Well, that's how – by holding back for a moment your response to outer influences, suggestions, opinions, facts and calling on the Light from within to reveal to you the right (or righteous) response to those opinions, facts, suggestions.

Denial is an important principle. It not only enables you to dissolve previously programmed false beliefs, but it acts as strong-armed Doorman to keep unwanted, negative suggestions from entering your subconscious mind. For instance, when you find yourself identifying with symptoms in a Doctor's column in your newspaper, and by identifying I mean experiencing a "feeling" of fear or apprehension that you might have some of them or get some of them, say to yourself, "CANCEL." That is a short denial that closes the door. The destructive suggestion triggered by the article and nourished by your own compulsive negative response can't get in; it is stopped in its tracks.

You will find that DENIALS are particularly helpful in combatting strong, emotional feelings that are obviously negative or destructive.

For instance, if you are dreadfully afraid of something or someone so that you can almost taste the fear, somehow a DENIAL is like a David that stands up to the giant Goliath and says, "I see you, I am not minimizing your apparent size and strength, BUT I AM NOT AFRAID OF YOU.

Sometimes we can use prayer as an escape. When trouble looms that causes us to shake in our emotional boots, we run to a corner and pray. And too many times when our prayer time is over we go right back to shaking and fearing again.

Denial is facing the facts, the way David faced the armored giant, and with your slingshot of faith and its stones of TRUTH BELIEFS calmly, fearlessly, skillfully slaying the giant.

Actually the giant or the thing you feared is a projection of your own fear thoughts and imaginings. It is significant that David killed the giant by hitting him in his only weak spot – the forehead, which is metaphysically recognized as the seat of the IMAGINATION.

AFFIRMATIONS

Lesson Five

Denials, as we mentioned in the last lesson, break up, dissolve, and disintegrate limited and false beliefs in the subconscious mind.

Affirmations build, establish, and construct, new desirable, Truth-founded beliefs in your subconscious mind.

Before we go any farther, let's explain what is meant by a belief and why we emphasize or talk so much about "beliefs."

Webster defines a belief as "acceptance of something as true, trustworthy, real." Illustration: as a child you are told by a parent that if you get your feet wet you will catch an awful cold and get sick.

Because a parent is the highest and perhaps only authority figure in a child's world, you, the child, totally accepted this opinion as true, trustworthy, real. It was tucked away in your subconscious mind and every time you get caught in the rain you hustle to get your feet dry, and if you can't for some reason or other, you get the sniffles.

Now, that admittedly is an over-simplified example. You may say, "I remember my parents telling me that, but I don't fear getting a cold when my feet are wet." That may be true, but only because somewhere along the line you dissolved that belief, denied it. Perhaps you were an athlete and proud of your physical abilities and when your feet got wet the belief that you could catch a cold was over-powered by your stronger belief that physically you were a pretty remarkable person and a little rain or snow couldn't hurt you.

That, however, is only one little example. All of our lives we are picking up and plastering our subconscious with all kinds of "beliefs, or acceptance of opinions or suggestions as true, trustworthy, and real." Most of these are untrue, or limiting in nature, but they nevertheless are unseen "causes" that form and shape your life.

Outer conditions are effects, results – they are like an arrow that has been shot out of the bow. There is no calling it back; wherever the power you gave it when you let go of the bow string takes it – there it must inevitably go.

Your mental beliefs are causes. They determine where the arrow is going to go and give it the power to get there.

As a matter of fact, that makes a pretty good analogy. Let's develop it further. Visualize an archer shooting at a target some distance away. Instead of the usual numbered labels on the target it is divided into sections which read, "Failure," "Lack," "Never quite making it" and other sections labeled, "Winner," "Success."

Now this archer we are watching keeps taking aim and making direct hits in the negatively labeled areas. Boy, he can hit "Lack" and "Failure" on the nose every time!

"Look here," you tell him, "why don't you change your aim just a little and hit some of those sections that read, "Success" or "Winner?" You point out to him that whatever section he hits, he gets, or he experiences in his life.

So he tries. But he has developed such a habit pattern of aiming at the negative labels that almost automatically his muscles and fingers fall into the old groove and "whoosh" the arrow still hits a negative-labeled area.

After several disappointing tries, he gives up in disgust and says, "Leave me alone. It is so difficult to make the new adjustment in my aim, and the old way is so easy I can do it almost with my eyes closed."

And so you walk away, wishing there were some way you could make it easier for him to break the old habit and have the patience and courage to form a new one.

Mental beliefs are causes or the direction and power behind the arrow. Outer conditions are effects – the result of the direction and power given the arrow by your belief. You can't recall the arrow, you can't change the past; but you can choose to change your aim starting now!

O.K. let's talk about how you and I can start changing our aim. It doesn't come easy at first. As we pointed out in the analogy, the old thought patterns have become habitual and resist our attempts to change them. Remember when you changed from a car that had standard gearshift to one with an automatic gearshift, how you kept stamping your left foot down on an imaginary clutch? You would try not to, and would feel silly every time you did, but that old subconscious habit would defy you.

But here is the wonderful, freeing secret – you can change your subconscious mind. You can build whatever belief you choose into your subconscious mind and that belief will automatically out-picture on your "screen of life!"

The principle of building a new belief is called
AFFIRMATION.

AFFIRMATION means to "make firm," "to establish," "to BUILD."

Just as Denial washes away, dissolves, breaks up, so does Affirmation build, establish, make substantial.

To go back to our example of the automatic transmission, actually you used the principles of denial and affirmation. You said to yourself, "This car has no clutch. I do not have to raise my left foot (DENIAL). I will leave my left foot on the floorboard (AFFIRMATION)." This BUILDS a new subconscious response.

As you continue your study of Truth you will learn how to formulate affirmations or affirmative statements of Truth for specific circumstances or needs. However, in this basic lesson in Affirmations, Dr. Cady suggests four primary affirmations that lay the foundation, so to speak, for an entirely new approach to life and living.

The first is:

"GOD IS LIFE, LOVE, INTELLIGENCE, SUBSTANCE, OMNIPOTENCE, OMNISCIENCE, OMNIPRESENCE."

God is Life – the Life flowing in you and in me right this minute, is God, as Life!

God is OMNIPOTENCE. This means God is the Source of all power. (The prefix "omni" is from the Latin language and means, "all" – and "potence," of course, means "power." Omnipotence – all power.)

God is OMNISCIENCE. Again, omni means all; and science means "to know" or "knowing." God is ALL-KNOWING! All-Wisdom.

God is OMNIPRESENCE. Or, God is EVERYWHERE PRESENT. The Spirit and activity of God is everywhere, evenly present – in all places, at all times! Or, as the Bible says, "In Him we live, move, and have our being."

The Second all-inclusive affirmation is:

> *"I AM A CHILD OR MANIFESTATION OF GOD, AND EVERY MOMENT HIS LIFE, LOVE, WISDOM, POWER FLOW INTO AND THROUGH ME. I AM ONE WITH GOD AND I AM GOVERNED BY HIS LAW."*

Many of us have unwittingly accepted the belief that we are miserable sinners, worms of the dust, unworthy of any recognition from God because we have done what we think are some very bad things in the past.

Maybe we have, but God is a God of the NOW, not the past. God's forgiveness of past mistakes is as instant as your forgiveness of yourself – the old self, the unenlightened self who through vanity, selfishness or whatever made the mistake.

You are a child of God. Jesus taught that. You and I may make mistakes and do things we ought not to do, but that doesn't make us inherently a sinner. It only makes us a child of God who is mixed up, lost, has forgotten his royal, spiritual parentage.

> *"I AM A CHILD OR POINT OF EXPRESSION OF GOD, AND EVERY MOMENT HIS LIFE, LOVE, WISDOM AND POWER FLOW INTO AND THROUGH ME, I AM ONE WITH GOD AND GOVERNED BY HIS LAW."*

The third all-inclusive affirmation is:

> *"I AM SPIRIT, PERFECT, HOLY, HARMONIOUS, NOTHING CAN HURT ME OR MAKE ME SICK OR AFRAID, FOR SPIRIT IS GOD, AND GOD CANNOT BE SICK OR HURT OR AFRAID. I MANIFEST MY REAL SELF THROUGH THIS BODY NOW!"*

This, you see, is building a new belief more closely founded on the Truth. Jesus said that God is Spirit; you are a child of God, therefore your basic nature is also Spirit.

I think that too many of us equate the term "human being" with physical being. "We are a physical being, but the physical part of us is only about 2% of us. The rest is mental and spiritual." You are much more a mental, emotional, and what is most important, a SPIRITUAL BEING. In Unity, it is the Spiritual part of your beingness that we emphasize and look to!

The fourth all-inclusive affirmation is:

*"GOD WORKS WITH ME TO WILL AND TO DO
WHATSOEVER HE WISHES ME TO DO, AND
GOD CANNOT FAIL."*

Building this new and unlimited belief into your heart or subconscious
mind automatically places you in tune with divine guidance. It is like the
servo-mechanism in a rocket that unerringly guides it to its destination.
This affirmation belief automatically causes you to be in the right place at
the right time, to say or do the right thing in the right way.

FAITH

Lesson Six

If you think about it, the word FAITH cannot stand alone.

You must have faith IN something!

We take it for granted that when we say, "I have faith" that we mean faith IN GOD. But it is right at this point that we need to check ourselves and say what we mean.

Have you ever heard someone say, "I have faith, but . . ." And then they go on to list in a tearful and forlorn voice all of the obstacles, all of the problem circumstances and problem people involved in their painful situation.

If we would learn to say, "I have faith . . . in God," instead of fooling ourselves that we are implying the words, "in God" when we say, "I have faith . . .," we might get the shock of our lives. For when you say "I have faith in God" how can you possibly give any serious consideration to any apparent obstacles or problem people? Does not the word, God, automatically mean you are speaking about a Power and Presence and Wisdom that is superior to any circumstance or person that your human intellect considers threatening?

This is a very important point because failing to actually say or at least, inwardly say the words, "faith IN GOD" the direction of our faith can be easily turned toward what we have feared, and bring that which we have feared into our experience.

Faith is a power. It empowers whatever belief you attach to it with the ability to become visible. When you say, "I have faith, but . . . I really can't see how in the world this problem can be successfully worked out . . ." and then you go on to state or inwardly contemplate all the things you have tried and haven't worked out, and how the problem is draining your strength so that you don't know how you are going to go on; then your faith isn't directed at a belief in God at all, it is directed at a belief that this problem is bigger than you are and therefore you are done, finished, beaten.

But if you get in the habit of looking at your problem experiences and then saying or thinking, "I have faith IN GOD," you will find that it is almost impossible to add any "buts." Adding a "but . . ." graphically, dramatically points out your basic hypocrisy. The only thing that can follow the statement, "I have faith in God" is a period, or perhaps an exclamation point for emphasis.

Jesus points out this subtle danger in the word faith in a well-known verse from Mark. The verse is usually quoted and memorized like this:

> *"Truly, I say to you, whoever says to this mountain, 'Be taken up and cast into the sea,' and does not doubt in his heart, but believes that what he says will come to pass, it will be done for him."* (Mark 11:22)

The passage, just as I have quoted it, and the way most people think of it, is intended to point out the power of faith – not necessarily the power of "faith in God," but just the power of faith to bring about whatever BELIEF it is directed at or attached to.

In this particular illustration the power of faith is directed at the belief that a mountain would be taken up and moved into the sea.

But if you will notice in your Bible, the complete verse reads:

> *"And Jesus answered them, 'Have faith in God. Truly I say to you, whoever says to this mountain, 'Be taken up and cast into the sea,' and does not doubt in his heart, but believes that what he says will come to pass, it will be done for him."*

In other words, He is saying that the power of faith is tremendous, greater than we can ever imagine, and it will bring about whatever we direct it at, whatever we really believe in our hearts – SO, for goodness sake, make sure your faith is directed at a belief in God!

Jesus concludes that little private teaching to his intimate friends and disciples with the statement:

> *"Therefore I tell you, whatever you ask in prayer, believe that you receive it, and you will."*

This, you might say, is His "how to do it step." He told them of the tremendous power of faith. He cautioned them to make sure that faith was in God.

Then, in the privacy of prayer, state your need and depend entirely, unquestionably, completely on God to fulfill it and Jesus flatly states, it will be fulfilled.

Now, let's go a little bit farther. It might be a bit difficult for some of us to accept or understand the words, "Have faith in God." What is God; Who is God? We ask.

We tried to answer those questions in a previous lesson entitled STATEMENT OF BEING. God is Spirit; everywhere present, always present, all-power, all-wisdom and so on.

But in this lesson on FAITH, it might be well to focus in on the aspect of God as operating through spiritual laws.

It admittedly might be difficult to have faith in a concept of God: as Spirit, invisible to the senses, "I have only your word," you might "I have only a vague feeling within me that what you say God is, is true. It is difficult to have complete faith and unquestioning dependency on a mere theory or feeling."

However, it is much easier to have faith in a law that we can observe operating, and that we can operate ourselves!

Illustration:

> If there could be a situation in which you had a class of students who had never heard of the concept of gravity. You could tell them the theory till you were blue in the face – explain it with diagrams, quote authorities who testified to its existence – and your students might still scratch their heads and say, "I think I understand."

> But then tell them each to hold a book out at arm's length – and then let go of it. As it dropped to the floor you would say, "There is the concept of gravity in expression."

They might insist, "But what is it? How does it work? What makes it drop? And you would honestly answer. "We don't know exactly what it is, all we know is that if you fulfill, or provide certain conditions, such as letting go of a book in midair, or of stepping out of a second story window, the law operates!"

So it is with God and God's universal spiritual laws. We may not know. intellectually why, for instance; when you give, it is given back to you full measure, pressed down, running over in your lap – which is the basic law of Supply taught by Jesus – but it works!

You can see then, that there is a corollary to faith in God; in order to activate that potential power, you must learn to provide the proper conditions, to fulfill the requirements of the laws through which God or Spirit expresses or operates.

For instance, there is a universal principle or law which one might call THE LAW OF THE VACUUM, because it works the same way as the familiar law of the vacuum that you learned about in your high school Physics class. You remember, if you pump or draw air out of a container, in time the container will burst from the pressure of the air trying to get in to replace what you have taken out.

Try this experiment in the same spirit that you asked your students in that class on gravity to try the experiment of letting go of a book and seeing what would happen:

> Try getting rid of, giving away, cleaning out or whatever, all the accumulated things in your house or office or desk that you have no further use for – that have served their purpose and are just lying around because you either are too busy or too lazy to throw them out – or that you hang on to, through some compulsive feeling of possessiveness (which is a nice word for the un-nice word, greed).
>
> As you do this, think of the Dead Sea. When water keeps flowing in and there is no outlet, the sea becomes putrid and no fish, no life can exist in it. A house full of stagnant, unused, unproductive clutter is the outer reflection of a Dead Sea consciousness.
>
> Get things moving, circulating – and watch for yourself how things that you have always wanted, things that you presently need – are attracted effortlessly into your life and experience.

Well, let's sum up. Remember the first part of the lesson when we discussed the importance of adding, "IN GOD" when you say you have faith. "Faith in God." Otherwise, it is so very easy to kid yourself, thinking you are handling a situation spiritually because you SAID you had faith, but actually the "buts . . ." that followed your alleged statement of faith gave witness to a faith in appearances.

And then remember that there is a corollary to faith in God. It is your responsibility to provide the most favorable mental, emotional, and physical conditions for the universal laws of the spiritual realm to work.

You can't think sickness, and demonstrate health.

You can't fill your consciousness with states of irritation, anger, hatred, resentment; and demonstrate harmony and order.

Faith is a faculty of mind: a power of mind. It can be used or directed wisely or unwisely. You are the user or director of this power. If you look out at your world of effects and become entranced and panic stricken by a threatening array of facts, your faculty of faith is pointed in their direction and they grow into the fulfillment of your faith-filled fears.

However, if you look inward to the kingdom of power and Wisdom and Light and become entranced by Its Light, your faculty of faith becomes the channel for God to express into your outer environment as the perfect answer to your pressing need.

CHEMICALIZATION PERSONALITY and INDIVIDUALITY

Lesson Seven

In this chapter Dr. Cady takes time to explain several terms that are sometimes used in metaphysical books and writings.

The first is: Chemicalization

And the Second: Personality and Individuality

First let's discuss chemicalization. This is a very interesting subject. Dr. Cady states: "Did you ever put soda into sour milk, cider, or other acid fluid, and witness the agitation or excited action which takes place? One of the substances neutralizes the other, and something better results from the action. This is a good illustration of what sometimes takes place in the minds and bodies of people."

Dr. Cady goes on to explain that many times, not always, when a person first starts using affirmations of Truth everything will go fine for a while, then unexpectedly there will seem to be a reverse! Things may go quite badly and the Truth student wonders what in the world happened.

The reason for this is that the new beliefs which one has been affirming and meditating upon have begun to drop into the subconscious mind, and are meeting resistance there from the old, solidified, entrenched false and limited beliefs. An agitation results (much like the analogy of soda and an acid fluid that we just mentioned). However, after a short period the strong, spiritually oriented beliefs neutralize the limited beliefs and, as Dr. Cady states, "something better results from the action."

I had what I am sure is a definite example of this when Elizabeth and I started to tithe – back in 1948. After several false starts – by that I mean we would place our tithe money in a special envelope, but as we ran short of funds we would borrow from the tithe fund and put in an I.O.U. to God. Before long the I.O.U.'s added up to so much that we would call off the tithing program. After several of those false starts, we wrote to Silent Unity to pray with us that we would have the faith and the courage to make tithing a consistent part of our lives and finances.

This time we stayed with it and we have tithed ever since. But . . . about a month and a half after we started tithing, everything started going wrong! There seemed to be more extra expenses. You know, things that come up unexpectedly, such as the car needing repair, and, well, I have forgotten the details, but I remember that the crowning event was when our basement flooded and after working in water up to my knees to try to clear it, I finally had to call in a plumber and was handed a big bill.

I remember writing a letter to God about that. I actually did! Didn't mail it, of course. But I wrote out all the promises in the Bible about how God takes care of those who love Him . . . and said, "How come? How about that basement?"

And you know, God answered my letter! He answered in a sort of peace that came over me after I finished writing the letter and getting it all out of my system. Somehow, the resentment, the bitterness, the anger was all gone. From that point on things began to fall into Divine Order.

We have tithed ever since, and although we are not wealthy by the world's standards of a million dollar stock portfolio, Cadillacs, and winter homes in the Bahamas – yet we have never wanted for anything and have always lived comfortably and happily.

So if you are new to the New Thought about Christianity with its emphasis on the spiritual factor in life, its emphasis on the practicality of DEPENDING upon invisible spiritual Powers and Laws, instead of depending upon people and outer conditions – if you are new to this, and you run into a period when "agitated or excited action" takes place in your life – stay with it. Stay with your affirmations of Truth. Stand firm against those entrenched hypnotic suggestions that the "world of effects" has entranced you with. They don't want to give up their comfortable abiding place in you.

Remember, a "chemicalization" experience isn't bad, it is good. It is a quick way of breaking up those solidified false and limited beliefs in your subconscious mind and making the channel clear for the Wisdom, the Power, the restorative Life, and abundant Supply of Universal Mind, or God, to flow through you and into your life.

The second term that Dr. Cady explains in this chapter is PERSONALITY and INDIVIDUALITY. Or more precisely, the distinction between personality and individuality.

We will discuss it at greater length, but in a short sentence:

> Personality is the personal, changing self of you;
> individuality is the unchanging, eternal, divine Self
> of you.

Personality changes, individuality never changes. It is the God Self of you, the Christ in you, the idea of Perfect Man in you.

The word personality is from the Greek word "persona" which was a mask worn by actors in the amphitheater. An actor would change masks according to the part he was called on to play. Individuality then, would be like the actor behind the mask. No matter what different mask he had on, the actor behind the mask was the same person.

On the personality level of our being we wear many masks too, don't we. We may be one person at work, another person at home, still another person on the golf course, and still another person when an officer stops us for going through a stop sign!

It is odd, and significant that if several friends are asked to describe the same mutual friend, the descriptions vary so much that in some cases it might seem as if they weren't talking about the same person.

This mask-changing we do can be the source of a lot of inner tension and turmoil. We display a different face to different people according to what we think they expect us to be or what will make the most favorable impression; and we end up not knowing who we really are ourselves!

There are many good things about my job, but one of the challenging things is trying to be myself when people unconsciously expect me to be like their mental image of a minister. But this is not unique with me. No doubt you too find yourself in situations where you feel the pressure to conform to what other people expect. And you ask yourself, "How should I act? What mask shall I put on so that I will be accepted by this particular group?"

This chapter on Personality and Individuality is the key to ending the game of masks. It points out that there are these two aspects to the self; the changing human personality and the changeless, perfect individuality.

> IF YOU CAN LIVE IN A CONSCIOUSNESS
> OF YOUR UNCHANGING
> INDIVIDUALITY, OR THE DIVINE SELF
> WITHIN YOU – THEN AUTOMATICALLY,
> EFFORTLESSLY, UNCONSCIOUSLY YOUR
> INDIVIDUALITY WILL MORE AND MORE

SHINE THROUGH YOUR PERSONALITY,
TO ENRICH AND IMPROVE IT.

In other words, be yourself – accept yourself – just as you are – with all your shortcomings and faults and flaws. For who of us is perfect? But, be faithful to your times of meditation. Dwell often on the idea that within you is the patterned idea of Perfect Man – just as within the acorn and the sapling oak is the patterned idea of a perfect oak tree. And that patterned idea is slowly, patiently, imperceptibly motivating you from within and changing you into its likeness.

As you do this you find your personality changing for the better in a way that is good and right; for you are letting the Light and Wisdom of Spirit change you instead of trying to do it yourself.

There are schools and books on personality improvement, which, for the most part are based on changing your outer behavior, changing your masks. But when you get home at night after a hard day of winning friends and influencing people, you find it a relief to take off your mask.

However, when you work from the Christ within, the change may be imperceptible from month to month, but it is permanent and natural. There is no taking off the mask, because you ARE that changed person.

An understanding of this distinction between personality and individuality is helpful, too, in cases where you are overwhelmed by or afraid of another's personality. That is, someone who always seems to say or do things that make you feel small or stupid, insecure, or afraid.

The next time you are in the presence of such a person, take a moment to look through or past his mask, his personality. See the individuality, the Son of God, God's perfect Idea of Man in him. Then, as the "mask" he is either purposely or unconsciously wearing – the mask of an overbearing or dictatorial personality – as this mask rages or smirks or whatever you will find it has no more effect on you than the frightening masks the little urchins wear on Trick or Treat night.

To sum up – the point is – be yourself. Accept yourself AS YOU ARE remembering that AS YOU ARE also includes the fact that you are a child of God – an individualized expression of the Universal Presence and Activity of God.

Individuality in you is "the Light that lighteth every man that entereth the world." You LET this Light shine ever more brightly when you live in the consciousness that God and you are one – that man is God in individualized expression.

SPIRITUAL UNDERSTANDING

Lesson Eight

In previous lessons we have been learning some of the principles of the Unity way of interpreting Jesus' teachings. We learned about the nature of God as SPIRIT: and our similar nature as children of God.

We learned about the function and power of thought or thinking and how our minds are the connecting points between ourselves and God.

We learned about denials and affirmations as mental tools with which we dissolve limited and false beliefs from our subconscious minds, and build new. Truth-oriented, God-oriented beliefs into that same subconscious – or as the Bible refers to it, the heart. "As he (man) thinketh in his heart, so is he."

We learned about our faculty of Faith which reaches right into the invisible Substance of God and brings forth into form the fulfillment of our needs and good desires.

Last week we discussed the interesting phenomenon of "chemicalization," which sometimes results when affirmations of Truth neutralize the entrenched limited and false beliefs in our subconscious. Also the distinction between the changing personality, and the unchanging INDIVIDUALITY of you and of me.

Now in this lesson Dr. Cady gives us a glimpse of the goal toward which all these principles and techniques point – the goal of spiritual understanding.

Spiritual understanding is not to be confused with intellectual knowledge, although it usually IS confused with intellectual knowledge.

The difference is that one comes to you from outside yourself – from books, lectures, the opinions of teachers or people whom you consider to be authority figures. Actually, it is INFORMATION rather than knowledge. You read, listen to others, and after a while you begin to believe that the ideas are yours, that they came from you. But actually they are suggestions and opinions that you have accepted from others.

Not only can you fool others when all you have is intellectual information about Truth; but the sad part is you fool yourself. And you only realize you have been fooling yourself when the real spiritual understanding comes and you see the other for what it was – information, a lot of facts, opinions, a large and ready vocabulary of words about the subject.

Spiritual understanding is that which arises from within. It can only happen when you have dug the "wells" within through frequent periods of inner stillness, silence, meditation, meditative prayer or whatever term you want to use for the act of getting quiet, going within, and listening, waiting, desiring, yearning for Understanding.

I imagine many of you have read the Old Testament and are familiar with the many passages that talk about Wisdom and Understanding.

"With all thy getting, get understanding."

What do you suppose that meant? What did it or does it mean to you as you read those passages? Do you skip over them quickly thinking that they mean just what you are doing – reading the Bible, getting lots of information about the Bible – knowing the Bible so well that you can turn to a little known part like the Book of Joel or Micah without having to look up where it is in the index in the front the Bible?

Don't ever be envious of someone whom you feel is much more acquainted with the Bible than you are from this academic or informational point of view. They may have more knowledge of biblical facts, but it doesn't prove they have spiritual understanding.

The Bible is pointing the reader toward something – toward an individual realization of God as both a universal Presence and an indwelling, personal Presence – and once that Understanding arises or happens in you all the words that "talk about" that realization become clear and simple.

In Matthew 16 we have a graphic illustration of spiritual understanding "happening" in an individual.

> *Jesus is talking with several of His friends and disciples and He asks them, "Who do men say that the Son of man is?" And they all contributed an answer out of their intellectual information by saying, "Some say John the Baptist, others say Elijah, and others Jeremiah or one of the prophets,"*
>
> *Then Jesus says, "But who do YOU say that I am?" In other words, those are the opinions of others – O.K. now, reach within yourselves for the Light of Understanding to reveal to you the answer.*

All were quiet – when suddenly Peter blurted out, "You are the Christ, the Son of the living God!"

This was not information that came from a book or a teacher, this was a flash of Understanding that suddenly illumined Peter's mind from within.

And Jesus quickly turned to Peter, and we could imagine a smile of relief and joy on His face as He said, "Blessed are you, Simon Bar-Jonah! For flesh and blood has not revealed this to you (that is, it didn't come from the outside – from a book or person), but my Father who is in heaven."

In other words, it came from within – it arose, bubbled up from the silent spiritual depths where each of us is eternally united with Universal Mind, or Spirit.

Then Jesus went on to say, "And I tell you, you are Peter and on this rock I will build my church and the powers of death shall not prevail against it."

"On this rock I will build my church . . ." On what rock? On Peter, the man? No, on the Understanding that Peter experienced the understanding that Jesus was more than the flesh and blood man that Peter saw before him; beyond that, Jesus was the embodiment of the one Christ, the one Pattern Idea of perfect man that God created and that indwells every person.

In short, Jesus' Church is built on Spiritual Understanding and that Church still exists – crossing the boundaries of denominationalism, crossing the boundaries of all religions. Those who come into a realization of the spiritual dimensions of life through an inner revelation, an inner awakening, are of the one Church.

In trying to describe spiritual understanding I may have seemed to "put down" intellectual knowledge, study and information. But this was only to make clear the goal toward which the seeker should be headed. Actually intellectual knowledge and information is very important at the beginning of the journey.

John the Baptist represents intellectual knowledge. John had to come first. John prepared the way for Jesus. Even as your Bible study and Truth study prepare the way for spiritual understanding.

John cried out in the wilderness. The wilderness symbolizes your imprisonment to the world that your five senses constantly report to you. You have been exposed to, attached to, depended on, pinned your faith on the outer world of parents, schools, jobs, business cycles, statistics, – the whole bit – for so long that you are lost confused, hungry and lonesome.

Then along comes John, or an intellectual knowledge of Truth – perhaps through a book you read, a lecture, a friend, even a radio program. You study more and all your study tells you "ABOUT" a Power, a Potential. If you keep on studying and reading you know all ABOUT God and ABOUT man's relationship to God but you don't necessarily KNOW God, and KNOW your relationship to God. This KNOWING, as differentiated from KNOWING ABOUT – is spiritual understanding.

So, to sum up the steps to spiritual understanding as well as I am able to sum them up through words – which again, is intellectual, or from outside of you:

> The first step is study. John the Baptist comes first. You must be discontent with things the way they are. You must feel that there is another and better way to live. You must get a working knowledge of the spiritual principles and concepts that Jesus taught.
>
> Then comes DESIRE. You must desire spiritual understanding with all your heart. Not halfhearted, not as a hobby, not as a tool or technique to get what you want. Your desire must be so deep and engrained, that if you don't get your desire right away you don't even think of giving up – you keep on hungering and thirsting, as Jesus put it, for this understanding.
>
> Simultaneously with DESIRE comes meditation or going within. If you want groceries you go to a grocery store; if you want a book you go to the library, if you want an experience of God, if you want understanding and Wisdom from the universal Pool of Wisdom – where else do you go but within!

One more thing that promotes your progress toward that goal of spiritual understanding is using the Truth Principles that you presently intellectually understand. By this I mean the day by day, hour by hour working at being aware of an invisible Power and Presence that interpenetrates this visible veil of environment.

Practice being an observer to what happens to you and around you, instead of completely identifying yourself with the psychological and emotional states that come into your field of consciousness as a compulsive reaction to what people say or do. Take that split second to open yourself to inner direction. In short, ACT, DON'T REACT!

Act from the guidance of the Light within you, instead of compulsively reacting the way the outer condition or person tempts you to do.

THE SECRET PLACE OF
THE MOST HIGH

Lesson Nine

This lesson is entitled, THE SECRET PLACE OF THE MOST HIGH. and it deals with the mystical place, deep within, where the Spirit of God meets and mingles with its individuated expression – you!

First, where does the term, Secret Place come from?

Well, it comes from the Bible. The 91st Psalm begins with the words:

> *"HE THAT DWELLETH IN THE SECRET PLACE OF THE MOST HIGH SHALL ABIDE UNDER THE SHADOW OF THE ALMIGHTY."*

"Under the shadow of the Almighty," what does that mean; Much of the Holy Land is barren desert. I flew over miles and miles of such land when I visited the Holy Land. In this desert, shade can sometimes mean the difference between life and death. So the writer of Psalms used this metaphor to dramatically bring out the dwelling in a consciousness of oneness with God will give you the same feeling of peace and security that you would experience if you had trudged weary miles through barren desert and then came upon oasis and a grove of trees.

How many times have you and I gone through experiences when the pressure of challenging events coming at us one after another drained our strength and we wondered how we could ever go on? That need happen to you no more. You are learning of a Secret Place that you can go to at any time, under any circumstances and find shelter, refreshment, and new strength.

Further along in the Psalm we find that classic verse:

> *"A THOUSAND MAY FALL AT YOUR SIDE, TEN THOUSAND AT YOUR RIGHT HAND; BUT IT WILL NOT COME NIGH THEE."*

This is the spiritual promise and spiritual Law of Protection. Bible Promises are really spiritual Laws. Notice, the promise is a conditional one: IF you dwell in the Secret Place THEN drastic things may happen all around you, but they will not hurt or harm YOU. This is exactly the way all laws are stated: IF you provide such and such conditions, THEN such and such results will follow. If you DO NOT fulfill those conditions, the law will not operate, the promise will not be fulfilled. You will not receive the result you desire.

At any rate, I have seen this spiritual Law of Protection work in the lives of innumerable people. For instance, a man of 57 was thrown out of work. From all sides arose the "they say" voices, saying that he was done for and would be lucky to get any kind of work. This man used affirmative prayer and sought the Secret Place in times of meditation and miraculously was guided into a position that he enjoyed even more than his old work, and it paid more!

Toward the end of the 91st Psalm we are given our first clues to the Secret Place of the Most High:

> *"BECAUSE HE CLEAVES TO ME IN LOVE, I WILL DELIVER HIM: I WILL PROTECT HIM, BECAUSE HE KNOWS MY NAME: WHEN HE CALLS TO ME, I WILL ANSWER HIM."*

Clue number one is: "Because he cleaves to me in LOVE!"

I suggest that the word, Love, as used here, means more than worship or adoration – it means that, too, but it also means more. It means that you TOTALLY ACCEPT THE BELIEF THAT GOD IS – THAT THE PRESENCE AND ACTIVITY OF THE UNIVERSAL CREATIVE SPIRIT THAT WE CALL GOD – IS A FACT, IS AN ABSOLUTE REALITY!

Clue number two is: "Because he cleaves to me in love, I will deliver him. I will protect him, because he knows my NAME!"

Clue number two is God's name! What is God's Name?

It isn't God, or Jehovah, or The Almighty. These are descriptive titles for the Deity.

God's Name is I AM! This is revealed in the Bible when Moses asked God what God's Name was. Remember, Moses said, "Who shall I say sent me, if the children of Israel ask me?" And God answered, "I AM THAT I AM. Tell them I AM sent you!"

If you take time to think it through you will find that the statement, I AM THAT I AM, means GOD IS THE UNIVERSAL BEINGNESS, OR

UNIVERSAL I AM WHICH FINDS EXPRESSION IN EVERY PERSON AS THAT PERSON'S SENSE OF "I AM!"

In other words, when you whisper to yourself, "I AM," you are speaking both God's Name and your own real, spiritual Name. God is the universal I AM that expresses in you and as you, as your personal sense of I AM!

When you say, "I am calm, confident, and vitally healthy!" you are using God's Name, you are saying "God – or God in me – is calm, confident, and vitally healthy – which is the Truth, isn't it!

On the other hand, you use God's Name in vain when you make a statement such as: "I am tired, weak, a miserable failure at all I do." If God's Name is I AM, this is saying God in you is tired, weak, a failure which is not only obviously false, but places you out of tune, out of phase, with the Divine Impulse and your careless or ignorant words lead to increasing weakness – just the way a careless short circuit burns out the wires of a motor.

Jesus said, "By thy words thou shalt be justified and by thy words thou shalt be condemned." (Matt. 12:37) You can now see why this is so. When you attach a negative word to I Am, you are bringing on your own downfall.

We can see now that this SECRET PLACE OF THE MOST HIGH cannot be any other place but within man, within you, and within me. Right here at the very center of your being; hidden within the very folds of that feeling of I AMness – or your basic sense of being, being alive, being you – here is where you are one with God, and where you experience the Presence and Power of God.

In his letter to the Colossians, Paul wrote: "This is the mystery which has been hidden for ages and generations, but is now revealed; Christ in you, your hope of glory!" (Col. 1:26, 27)

Christ in you means the universal Idea of perfect Man, which God created in the beginning and implanted in each person in THAT SECRET PLACE OF THE MOST HIGH!

Through Christ, or through that God-Idea or perfect Man, implanted in the innermost heart of you, you can do all things – if you step aside and not only "let" but DEPEND on the Wisdom and direction of your indwelling Christ.

Dr. Cady, in the book, Lessons in Truth, points out that this Secret Place of the Most High, this hidden place where Christ abides in you in all fullness, is not reached by the road of the intellect alone.

Intellectual understanding, and by this we mean reading books, listening to teachers, writing correspondence school lessons on Truth principles; does not guarantee a personal revelation of the Secret Place in you.

"This revelation," Dr. Cady writes, "Will never come through the intellect of man to the consciousness, but must ever come through the intuitional to the intellect as a manifestation of Spirit to man."

Intellectual study of Truth, including reading these Truth lessons – is like traveling a road that leads to the boundary of the kingdom of God within you – but there comes a time and a place when you must walk alone. And when you do, you will find that you are not alone, you are never alone. The Christ at the center of your being is your strength, your guide, your protector, and your comforter.

Finding and dwelling in The Secret Place of the Most High is, of course, a mystical experience. Christianity, at its core, is a mystical religion.

Webster defines Mystical: "Neither apparent to the senses nor obvious to the intellect. Derived Immediately, rather than mediately; based on intuition, insight, or similar subjective experience."

When Jesus was called before Pilate He assured Pilate that His kingdom was not of this world; that is, it wasn't apparent to the senses. Yet in several places Jesus states that the kingdom of God is "At Hand." In other words, the kingdom of God exactly fits Webster's description of a mystical experience, "neither apparent to the senses, nor obvious to the intellect. Derived Immediately, rather than mediately." Mediately means through a mediator – which could be a teacher or book; Immediately means directly, without outer assistance.

Remember, Jesus told His followers that He must go, and the Spirit of Truth would come to teach them. The Spirit of Truth is an inner Teacher. The disciples were looking too much to Jesus with His outstanding and radiant personality. He knew that He must go so that they would be forced to look within and let the Spirit of Truth guide them to their own secret place of the Most High and to even deeper Truths that they weren't as yet able to understand.

Friends, there is a kingdom, a dimension, a very real and present environment which is NOT apparent to your five senses, not obvious to your intellect. There is, as Jesus sincerely taught, an inner Teacher, the

Spirit of Truth, which will reveal to you personally the deeper things of this realm. But in order to become awakened to this kingdom and to the instruction of the Spirit of Truth you simply must attempt to break out of your unceasing preoccupation with, dependence on, and fear of the external world that your five senses report to you and spend time in meditation seeking, hungering and thirsting after, the kingdom that is not of this world, yet is at hand, even within you.

FINDING THE SECRET PLACE

Lesson Ten

Jesus promised,

> *"Truly, truly, I say to you, he who believes in me will also
> do the works that I do; and greater works than these will
> he do, because I go to the Father."* (John 14:12)

Where will we get this power to "do the works" that Jesus did; "and greater works" than He did? It stands to reason that we will get it from the same place that Jesus got it – from the universal Creative Spirit that indwells and enlivens all persons. We call this Universal Creative Spirit, God; Jesus called it, The Father – His Father, our Father.

So now let us ask ourselves, "What do I do? How do I make contact with this indwelling Power of which Jesus speaks?"

The way that Unity suggests is the spiritual technique of Meditation, or what is sometimes called, "The Silence." It is patterned after Jesus' instructions concerning prayer when He said:

> *"And when you pray, you must not be like the hypocrites;
> for they love to stand and pray in the synagogues and at the
> street corners, that they may be seen of men. Truly, I say to
> you, they have their reward. But when you pray, go into
> your room and shut the door and pray to your Father who
> is in secret, and your Father who sees in secret will reward
> you."* (Matthew 6:5)

So the first step in meditation, or The Silence, is to go apart someplace "*In your room and close the door,*" Jesus suggests. Or it could be a certain quiet, private spot in your backyard, or on a secluded bench or even a boulder in a park. The idea is that you be alone and free from as many distractions as possible.

Once you have found the suitable physical place, the next step in meditation is to RELAX your body, your mind, and your emotions.

First your body. I many times find myself beginning a time of meditation with a big sigh! Try it! As the breath from the sigh goes out, you seem to relax all over. Then, kind of check your body – are your hands relaxed?

Sometimes it may be good to shake your hands vigorously, shake them as though you were trying to shake your hands right off your arms! When you stop you will feel your fingers and hands are much more relaxed and tension free.

Another tension point is your upper shoulders. Move your shoulders around a little bit, loosen up those muscles – relax them, settle down into your body!

Now, relax your mind, or your thoughts. Our minds are like a busy street, people milling about, cars turning every which way, horns blowing, buses maneuvering in and out! But it isn't like that all the time. Visualize a downtown section at 3 a.m. – quiet, peaceful, the streets deserted. Now let your mind be like that – quiet, peaceful, serene, resting.

The best way to quiet your emotions is to breathe slowly and rhythmically. You might be upset over something someone said to you, or about you. Or you might be frightened about some threatening circumstances in your life. But you will find that if you just consciously breathe slowly and deeply, those tempestuous emotions will quiet down (even as the Sea of Galilee quieted when Jesus spoke the words, *"Peace, be still!"*)

The next step in meditation, or the Silence, is to follow the advice of Hosea and *"Take with you words, and return to the Lord."* (Hosea 14:2)

Nature abhors a vacuum. And when you attempt to empty and quiet your mind and thoughts, you will find all kinds of miscellaneous images and thoughts coming in: a conversation you had with someone yesterday; a thought of something you have to purchase, or a letter you should write. You can prevent this by consciously directing your thoughts to a Bible passage – perhaps the Twenty-third Psalm, or the Lord's Prayer.

Following the Lord's Prayer or some similar Bible verse, work with an affirmative statement of Truth, or what we call an affirmation. For instance, this simple one:

"GOD IS MY HELP IN EVERY NEED."

Repeat it. Think about it. What does it mean? Start with the first word – God. Who or what is God? "God is Spirit," you answer to yourself. "God is the universal Creative Spirit and Activity that is moving in and through all things. God's Spirit is moving through the birds whose happy, chirpings fall upon my ears right now. God's Spirit is moving in and through the people that I hear in the distance or going by in cars. God is everywhere-present Spirit and that Spirit is filling me now – living through me and expressing AS me!

Then go on to the second word of the affirmation – IS. "God IS my help in every need." Is means right now. Is doesn't mean "was" nor does it mean, "will be." It means "is" – Now! Right now God IS with me. Right now God IS moving in my body and affairs to establish divine order and harmony, to guide me into right action. There is nothing to fear.

The third word is – MY. "God is MY help in every need." Meditating on this word will serve to bring to mind the personal relationship between your indwelling Father and you. God may be a universal Presence and Power, but as you reach inward to God through the Secret Place of the Most High, God becomes your personal, loving Father, or Lord.

Dr. Cady in the book LESSONS IN TRUTH writes:

> "There is one Spirit, one Father of all, in us all, but there are different manifestations or individualities. Your Lord is He who will deliver YOU out of all your troubles. Your Lord has no other business but to manifest Himself to you and through you, and so make you mighty with His own mightiness made visible; whole with His health."

And thus you go on with each word of an affirmation. "God is my HELP in every need." Help, that is just exactly what you need, isn't it. Life is confusing, life is challenging, life is at many times overwhelming. We can't handle it alone; it is too much for us. But we weren't meant to handle it alone! The Bible, and particularly the Teachings of Jesus, reveals that the Creative Spirit has not left Its offspring, you and me, helpless. We read,

> *"The eternal God is thy refuge, and underneath are the everlasting arms."* (Deut. 33:27)

And in the Psalms,

> *"He will not suffer thy foot to be moved, he that keepeth thee will not slumber."* (Psalm 121:3)

Yes, God is your very real, very present HELP in EVERY NEED!

> But now, what about the third step in meditation – the Silence Itself? Well, let me tell you something about the Silence – you have been "in" it all along! You are in it now!

The silence isn't something that comes and goes, or starts and stops. The Silence is continually "underneath," so to speak, all sound, all activity. It is just that you haven't been aware of it – even though it has been there all the time. It reminds me of a picture someone once showed to me. At first glance it looked like a lot of ink blots. I was assured there was a face of Jesus in the picture. I couldn't see the face, however. Others in the room looked at it and one by one they would say, "There, I see it!" Still, it was just some ink blots to me. The others tried to explain the features of Jesus to me. It was so very plain to them, but not to me. Suddenly, in a flash, I saw the face! And after once seeing it, it is never again hidden from you, it jumps out at you immediately.

That's how it is with this ever-present Silence. It has been here all the time, but you haven't been aware of it. Even when it is pointed out to you, you may not, at first, be able to "see" it. But suddenly, you will and from then on The Silence will no longer be a mystery, but a very tangible fact of life.

You will become aware that The Silence is like an ocean. The words you hear and the words you speak are like objects floating on the surface of the ocean of Silence. Even the thoughts you think are supported by the ocean of Silence.

We say, "The silence was broken by the sound of a child's voice." But the silence was not actually broken. The silence continued to exist, it is just that the sound waves of a child's voice struck your eardrum and took your attention from, or drowned out the ever-present Silence.

So, with this understanding of the Silence, the Silent Spirit and Activity of God, everywhere present we can see that the Silence isn't so much something we "enter," it is something we "Become conscious of," something we can experience at any time, in any place, under any circumstance. And it is from this Silence, and through YOUR AWARENESS OF IT – whence comes your Power. The Power of which Jesus spoke when He said, *"The things that I do, shall ye do also, and greater things shall ye do."*

As we come to the close of this lesson on Finding the Secret Place, listen to the Silence. Listen to it . . . in between . . . the very words . . . I . . . write . . . and . . . you . . . read.

All through the day take time to become consciously aware that underneath the sounds and your thoughts . . . is . . . The Silence.

SPIRITUAL GIFTS

Lesson Eleven

In chapter eleven of the book, LESSONS IN TRUTH, Dr. Cady makes the following observation:

> "What we all need to do above everything else is to cultivate the acquaintance or consciousness of Spirit within our own being. We must take our attention off results, and seek to live the life. Results will be 'added unto' us in greater measure when we turn our thoughts less to the 'works' and more to embodying the indwelling Christ in our entire being."

In the beginning many, if not most people become interested in the study of Truth because of what we might call the "loaves and fishes." That is, they have a specific and desperate need – perhaps for healing, or the loss of a loved one has left them desolate, or a particular emotional problem is tearing them apart.

They apply the teachings to their own specific problem with a great deal of success. Then there comes a time when the Unity student begins to catch sight of a larger vision. He understands that God is more than willing to give him the "loaves and fishes," or to abundantly fulfill his daily needs and heart desires – but he begins to see, too, that Jesus is talking about something more than a Divine Supermarket, Jesus is talking about a Way of Life, a Way of Living!

A Way of Living in which the thought that God is Spirit and you are an individualization of that universal Spirit, is constantly in the back of your mind, and in back of everything you do; every decision you make. I will always remember how one little word opened up an entirely new dimension of living for me. That word is, "AS."

One day a Unity speaker said, "God is expressing through you, and AS you!" "Through me" my mind accepted all right, but "AS" me! What did that mean?

While the speaker went on with other points, my mind was still back on the words, "AS me." That could only mean that God was or IS me, and conversely, I AM God. I can understand what a shock that might be to you, because it certainly was a shock to me. God IS ME, therefore, I am God in expression! But if you follow the implications of Jesus' teachings through to their natural conclusion, you cannot escape the fact that *GOD IS NOT ONLY EXPRESSING THROUGH YOU, BUT AS YOU!*

For instance, we are not little islands of life, neither do we have an individual energy cell within each of us wherefrom we receive that intangible, but very real thing that we call life or livingness. No, we agree that there is but One Universal Life or Life Force, and each of us is a point of expression of that One Universal Life. That Life is expressing through us, and AS us. We are one with It, and It is one with us – total unity, oneness, sameness.

That Universal Life Force is God, is it not? Therefore we are indivisibly one with God. Then when we remember that God is not only Universal Life (this is only one attribute of God's Spirit – although the one easiest to feel and understand and actually experience) – but God is also universal Love and Power and Wisdom and Substance and Beauty and Order. By the same logic, therefore, we are one with all these qualities that God is and we are potentially capable of expressing them, even as we are expressing God Life – to the limits of our present consciousness of God's Life.

This then, is when and where and how we get into the deep waters of Truth; the deep waters of Jesus' teachings. We seek not just to let God express through us as a healing Power to heal some personal physical need – and then kind of live the other areas of our life by our own wits; but we bring an awareness of God's presence into every act, every area of our lives. As we become used to living in these deeper waters of Truth, a funny thing happens, the "loaves and fishes," so to speak, no longer become as important as before! A specific challenge no longer is a goal to be attained, or an obstacle to be overcome – it becomes instead, an OPPORTUNITY to learn how to let God express through us more fully. It becomes an opportunity to grow spiritually, or grow in our consciousness of oneness with God!

At this point your whole viewpoint of life changes. It is what Jesus meant when He said you must be "born again." The first birth is the physical birth – and this refers not just to your physical body, but your mind or thinking is also physically oriented! You believe only in what you can see and touch, in the reports of your physical senses. Anything non-physical, or spiritual, is nonsense and foolishness to you. As Paul wrote in First Corinthians:

"The unspiritual man does not receive the gifts of the Spirit of God, for they are folly to him, and he is not able to understand them because they are spiritually discerned."

(I Cor. 2:14)

In the deep waters of Truth you begin to see that God is Universal Spirit and you are an individualization of that Universal Spirit, therefore It is you; and you are It. You then begin thinking past the limits of your physical senses. In addition to the first birth, or consciousness of the physical universe, you begin to acknowledge as just as real – the invisible, intangible spiritual universe, or as Jesus termed it – the everywhere present kingdom of God!

Then life really begins! Up to this time life was just a matter of getting by – of stumbling through each day always reaching for physical goals that never turn out to hold what you think they promise. For instance, to retire and get your long awaited pension, or to make a great sum of money, or to get your children through college.

Each goal, when attained, gave temporary satisfaction at best. And the first thing you know your string of days seems to be running out and you bitterly wonder what it is all about anyway.

But, with this larger understanding of your oneness with that universal transcendent Power that we call God, each day is new and exciting. Each year that rolls by makes you richer in spiritual know-how. You look forward to the future, whether you are 28 or 88, because you know that the Life that you are – is continuous and death is not an end, but it is an experience along the pathway of Life; just as birth is an experience along that same path.

Just as we grow physically, so are we designed with the potential to grow spiritually. The physical growth is more or less automatic; the spiritual growth requires our effort, our study, and most of all, our practice.

But just as it is exciting and satisfying to exercise daily, or jog daily, and see how we are growing into a stronger, healthier physical being – so is it infinitely more exciting and satisfying to practice living in a consciousness of oneness with God – and becoming aware of how you are more confident and serene; how your faith in God's Presence and help is becoming rock-ribbed and almost automatic.

Then of course, good things, nice things, exciting things keep happening to you, or are attracted into your life because you are getting into close harmony with the spiritual undercurrent of Order and Beauty and Harmony that governs the universe.

I know that you have heard this verse so many times that you might even think, "Oh, that again!" when I repeat it. But it bears repeating because it is the "deep water" answer to life. It is:

> "*And do not seek what you are to eat and what you are to drink, nor be of anxious mind. For all the nations of the world seek these things, and your Father knows you need them. Instead, seek His kingdom and His righteousness (or right action) and all these things will be yours as well.*"
>
> (Matt. 6:31)

Spiritual growth is seeking a greater awareness of the spiritual realm, the kingdom of God, in which we live, move, and have our being – and its right action, of course means the inner guidance, the inner motivation that is imparted to you from that inner kingdom.

Now there is one thing about growing that we should think about. Growth and change go together. Whether we are talking about the growth of a tree, or of a child, or of a business – where there is growth, there is change.

We stand in the way of our spiritual growth when we are afraid of change to the extent that we avoid or resist new experiences, new ways of doing things; new ideas.

Humanly we find a kind of comfort in tried and proven ways of living even though they may be boring, monotonous, and in some cases even painful. The comfort being that at least we don't have to go through the awful ordeal of change – of facing the unknown.

When your life takes a new turn, don't resist it. You have within you all the resources you need. You never attract anything to you that you aren't ready to handle if you handle it with Truth.

Unity has a saying, "When one door closes, another always opens!" And that's the Truth. So many persons spend the rest of their lives crying and whimpering on the doorstep of the closed door, longing for the "good old days" and missing the new and exciting wonders of the door that stands open and waiting!

The Bible says, "God is the giver of all good gifts," but the greatest of God's gifts – is the gift of Himself! May you be born into a new dimension of life as you meditate on the statement, "God is expressing through me and AS me!"

UNITY OF THE SPIRIT

Lesson Twelve

This lesson is called UNITY OF THE SPIRIT. In it Dr. Cady makes three points:

1. How all denominations and religions are striving for one goal.

2. How you can best help a loved one find God.

3. How God is both immutable Principle, AND loving Father.

First: ALL DENOMINATIONS AND RELIGIONS ARE STRIVING FOR ONE GOAL. And that goal is an understanding and an EXPERIENCE of the one God, the one Creative Principle, or whatever name we choose to call that FIRST CAUSE of all that is.

Picture in your mind a huge wheel with many spokes. Think of the spokes as people. Think of the rim or perimeter as representing the different churches, denominations, sects, religions. Think of the hub of the wheel as representing the One God, the one First Cause.

One person or "spoke" may be connected to the rim at an organization called Salvation Army. Another may be connected to the rim at a certain denomination. Another may be connected at a place called Buddhism.

> No matter at what point of the wheel the spokes start out – they end up at the Hub. Even so, no matter from what religious organization a person starts as he earnestly seeks God, as he moves toward the Hub – God, he becomes closer to every other spoke on the wheel until all meet at the Center.

Ecumenicity isn't necessarily brought about by organizations uniting at the "rim" of the wheel. Ecumenicity is automatically brought about as each person, each spoke, no matter what the label at his starting point seeks to grow in understanding and in the direct experience of God within him.

The second point is: HOW YOU CAN BEST HELP A LOVED ONE FIND GOD.

It is normal and natural for one who has discovered the spiritual dimension in life and witnessed Its power to transform, to want to introduce others, especially loved ones to this wonderful discovery.

Many of you have learned from experience how difficult this is. You can argue, you can send pamphlets, you can unknowingly make yourself obnoxious, but the loved one doesn't understand – might even resist and resent you.

Religion basically isn't an outer institution; it is a direction of mind. Until an individual chooses to take or try that direction of mind, any attempts to force him will only meet resistance and a "backing away."

I believe the very best way to help a loved one, or any person, to find God is to live, yourself, to your highest ability, a God-oriented life.

As YOU become more loving, more understanding – as you develop that spiritual serenity that enables you to take the storms of life without fear or panic or going to pieces – as you prosper through working with the prospering principles that God established to enable His progeny or children to prosper – as your life becomes transformed for the better, you will find your loved one, or ones, or friends, saying, "You're so changed. You don't seem to have any 'monkeys on your back' like other people. Things seem to work out so well for you. How do you do it? Tell me about it. What's your secret?"

Then is the time to plant the seed, to offer the pamphlet, to suggest the book, to invite them to your outer organization. And if they don't follow it up, don't be discouraged. You have planted a seed, and it will grow in its own time and place.

Meanwhile, your job is to behold the Christ in them; to behold the God-Self in them. Dr. Cady suggests the following prayer as an example or guide.

> *"THE HOLY SPIRIT LIVES WITHIN YOU: HE CARES FOR YOU, IS WORKING IN YOU THAT WHICH HE WOULD HAVE YOU DO AND IS MANIFESTING HIM SELF THROUGH YOU."*

The third point in this lesson is: HOW GOD IS BOTH IMMUTABLE PRINCIPLE AND ALSO A PERSONAL, LOVING FATHER.

Some persons, upon hearing Unity's emphasis on God as the Universal Principle of Goodness, think to themselves, "Well, what does this do to the Bible verses that speak of God as a warm, loving, understanding Father, Who cares for me personally?"

The answer is that God is both! In a sense we might say that "outside" of you God is immutable, undeviating Principle, but "within" you – or as everywhere present Principle finds an individualized point of expression in and through you – "It," becomes "He." Principle becomes personalized in you as your loving, indwelling Father-God.

As an analogy: take a tree, an apple tree. There is a Life-principle that is moving through the entire tree, giving life and growth to root, branch, twig, and leaf impartially, impersonally.

But let one leaf suffer harm, or one apple be bruised by a bird – and the impersonal Life-principle of the tree immediately becomes personal to that leaf or apple and works to heal it and fulfill its specific needs. Even so, God is universal everywhere present, all sufficient Wisdom and Love and Power. But when you appeal to this universal Principle for the fulfillment of a specific need, It or He immediately becomes personal to you.

Now, let's sum up the series. In doing this I would like to share with you a little habit I have developed over the years of reading many, many books.

I read the first paragraph of the book, and then the last paragraph of the book. In the very first paragraph an author tells you what he is going to say and why it needs to be said. In the last paragraph he tells you what he said, and how you can act on what he said. (At least that is what those two paragraphs should contain.)

Dr. Cady's first paragraph describes what needs to be pointed out to people and the general direction her book is going to take in fulfilling this need. She writes:

> "Every man believes himself to be in bondage to the flesh and the things of the flesh. All suffering is a result of this belief. The history of the coming of the Children of Israel out of their long bondage in Egypt is descriptive of the human mind, or consciousness, growing up out of the animal or sense part of man and into the spiritual part."

There is the problem, the need. Mankind has inherited a false and limited belief that the physical world of effects or form is all there is. If this is all there is, then we are dependent upon this outer world for our well-being (our health, our prosperity, our security, and so forth). What you are dependent upon you are enslaved to – in bondage to – and all our suffering results from this bondage.

Then the last paragraph of the book reads:

> "The whole business of your Lord (the Father in you) is to care for you, to love you with an everlasting love, to note your slightest cry, and to rescue you.
>
> Then you ask, 'Why doesn't He do it?' Because you do not recognize His indwelling and His power, and by resolutely affirming that He does now manifest Himself as your all-sufficiency, call Him forth into visibility. God is a present help in time of need; but there must be a recognition of His presence, a turning away from human efforts, and an acknowledgement of God only, (or the single eye) before He becomes manifest."

There is the answer or a recapitulation of what the author said and how you can act on what was said.

In other words, there is more to this universe than what your five senses report to you. They report an outer environment in which you live; but there is also an "inner environment" in which you live.

> Through realizing and acknowledging this inner environment or spiritual environment or God – you are able to recognize and in time – break through the inherited false belief that "the outer world is all there is and therefore you are completely dependent upon it."

When you see life and the universe in its wholeness; both the outer world of form and the inner world of Spirit – when you see the whole Truth, instead of just a part of the Truth – you switch your dependency from the world of form with its empty promises, to the realm of Spirit or as Jesus called it, the kingdom of God. And when your dependency is on God, your life is built on a rock foundation and every promise is kept, every need fulfilled.

You have a spiritual Man locked inside of you. A giant, a genius or whatever grand adjectives you can think of to describe this mighty One within you.

Through meditation and an earnest desire to free yourself from your bondage to the belief in a half-a-world – just the physical half – you release this spiritual Self and come to know true freedom, a sense of mastery, yet a sense of humility.

You understand through experience that there is no contradiction in the seeming contradictory statements:

> *"I of myself can do nothing . . ."*

> and

> *"All power has been given me in heaven and in earth."*
>
> (Matt. 28:18)

From then on you walk in the Light and from the Light. Life becomes altogether new, and meaningful. The Light analogy is a good one.

It is as if you had lived in a dark mansion all your life; suddenly lights are turned on all over.

It is a new world for you. You see beauty that the darkness obscured before. You see that things that were threatening obstacles in the dark, are easily handled in the light.

Yes, you have a new sense of freedom and mastery, but there is also that all-pervasive humility – for you know that it is the LIGHT not yourself that made this glorious new world possible.

A Meditation Based On Emily Cady's Five Attributes of God

After sitting quietly long enough to allow your racing thoughts to slow down to a tranquil pace . . .

picture yourself as being led by the invisible presence of God into a secret chamber down deep inside of you . . .

at one end is a throne upon which you feel you are invited to sit.

As you gaze around the chamber you see five arches leading into five rooms. One archway has the word LOVE inscribed across it, another WISDOM, and POWER, SUBSTANCE, LIFE.

A soft Voice fills the chamber saying,
"Beloved, what is your need? Do you see those five buttons on the arm of your seat of authority? Press the one that corresponds to the nature of your need, and then observe."

* * * * * * * *

Let's say your need is for   guidance on a certain matter.
You are confused, indecisive, worried . . .

You press the button marked, "WISDOM"
and a soft golden glow
fills that archway as you
find yourself saying with
utter faith and confidence

**"The Wisdom of God is inclining
me toward Right Action. I trust
in His intuitive guidance."**

(feel the hush of peace)

Or is healing your need? Is your bodily network of nerves bringing sensations of pain or other signals of fear-arousing symptoms?

Look toward the arch of LIFE
and as it glows you feel
the realization welling up
from within you that

**"The life of God fills me with
energy and wholeness."**

(relax)

In these days of inflationary prices and the emphasis on material objects as the hallmarks of success, it is easy to get uptight about finances and forget the true Source of the adequate and abundant Supply for your every need.

The word, SUBSTANCE, glows and
you feel your tension and
brow-wrinkling worry subsiding
as you remember:

**"The substance of God blesses
and prospers me."**

(all is well)

If your heart is troubled over many things and you find it difficult to know just what to ask for — the healing, harmonizing, prospering power of Love unlocks your answer.

**"The love of God is with me where
I am as my help in every need."**

Power means the ability to exercise authority; authority means the right to command, enforce laws, exact obedience.

You inherently have the right to exercise authority over your world of thoughts and feelings. By quickening the God-attribute of Power you develop the ability to wield your God given authority:

to command your thoughts, and to exact obedience from the cells of your body and the atoms of your environment.

The physical seat of the Power attribute is the throat. Place your center of attention at the throat as you affirm:

"The Power of God gives me authority over my mind, body, and affairs."

Benediction Thought:

"It was good to dwell in the inner chamber of the secret place of the Most High with the Christ 'I Am' on the throne of authority. I now re-enter the world of activity knowing that the power of God acts through me in all that I do."

I am grateful, Amen

NOTES

Made in the USA
Lexington, KY
09 March 2017